Roses Are Red
. . . and White

Roses Are Red
... and White

Poems
by
Jack Witt

For Rosalie & John
May the poems inspire your
own poetry.
Yours in friendship.
Jack Witt

BRANDYLANE PUBLISHERS
White Stone, Virginia

Artwork by Jack Witt.
Back cover photograph by Beth Agresta.

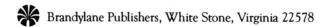 Brandylane Publishers, White Stone, Virginia 22578

Copyright 1996 by Jack Witt.
All rights reserved. Published 1996.
Printed in the United States of America.

Library of Congress Cataloging-in-Publication Data

Witt, Jack, 1934–
    Roses are red—and white: poems/by Jack Witt.
        p.   cm.
    ISBN 1-883911-08-7
    I. Title.
PS3573.I9154R67   1996
811'.54—dc20   96-13563
                                                                    CIP

This book of poems is dedicated to my wife Judy.

PREFACE

It's taken much of my adult life to write these ten short poems. Many of them have been in the making for over twenty years, and some will take revision even after they are in print.

The images are strong for me. Each of the flowers grow in my garden, either as weeds or as planted flowers. The cut bank, the wine jug, the polar explorer, each arose from feelings that were too strong to hold. They had to be worked out as poetry.

The poems fit together, for me, like coins in a set, each one with its own predestined space and there isn't room for any more in this book. I used color and calligraphy to try and make the poems pleasing to the eye and have deliberately presented them as though they were pages lifted from a medieval manuscript. It places them hopefully more firmly in the mainstream by enticing collective memory, atavism if you will, into the present. My wish for you who read this work is that these images, so much a part of my life, will enrich your own.

JW

roses are red
... and white

poems
by
jack witt

red roses

part I

Goshen

a poem of love

The leaves in the dogwood
reach Pale green and rose,
pale wings Their shades adja-
cent each The other lights,
complacent Where they meet
so that The other glows, does
not compete And thereby
doing so are Unopposed
complete.

Hollyhocks

a poem of
lasting things

Before the earth was garden
plots, There were a thousand
hollyhocks. Before a spade
cut through their hearts,
And the ground was border-
ed off with rocks. But ...
Ghostly flowers on phantom
stalks Fill our dreams, beco-
me our thoughts. Because
their purple-throated frocks
The deepest sense on earth un-
locks, Breaks up our gardens
rimmed with rocks And
flowers them with hollyhocks.

Morning Glories

a poem of goodbye

She has to pack up her
trunk Full of the non-clo-
thing she wore For a hand-
full of hours. Garments so
sheer, The blush they reveal -
ed Folded shyly Into what
had been shown- A star in
the translucent dawn
That disappears before
the hot rise touches the
few rumpled things She
has left behind ...

Her morning glory.

Mound

a poem of daemonic love

The grassy bank of a rutted
hill flourishes on the mound,
A carpet striped with gashes
made by rain rushing down.

The lusty turf unrolls in paths
of bladed coverlets.
Torrential storms cut deeply
with bloodly rivulets.

Virulent stalks thrust up-
ward, out, over cliffs of clay-
The vibrant green shoots, the
wounded red walls -
where lovers lay.

Wine Jug Heart

a poem of loss

When it happens—
when the grocery bag slips
and goes by your knees
causing "sudden stomach" to
jolt you – when the wine jug
hits the sidewalk with a
purple crash, and the bag
holding the skewered filets
Hleaks,

People are too nice to notice
when they know that
you've just dropped
your life!

Dandelions

a poem of passing

Dandelions – gone to seed. Lined
the edge of the hill where I stood. A
hund'ed heads were perfect thoughts
atop sunlit translucent stalks.
Silently, they stood, aware, Be-
coming wombs of woren air,
While hollow filamentous hearts,
Expected things to fall apart.
Look at the dandelion sphere!
Silver, round, almost not there –
A breath of twilight in her hair –
Waiting for a chance to
disappear!

... and white
part II

Swan

a poem of unattainable beauty

Hollow-boned for winter
flight, flesh-hidden, feath-
ered against the cold,
Her cool garments fold, un-
fold, reflecting sunlight
in flecks of gold.

Above, tall, she glides to
ponds, Where melting
snows run down for swans.

Wasp Nest

a poem of grief

On the coldest day of the win-
ter, he saw a ruin, tucked in a
frozen nook. And he picked it
like a flower out of the window
frame to get a closer look.
Compartments of stiff, grey paper
seemed to hold brittle air, and
frost-like ghosts in the dull sha-
dows huddled up there.
And he held the tuff nest the
wasps had made into a poem
book, trying to imagine how
they filled up the pages and
the lusty strength it took.

polar explorer

a poem of
purification

Sitting immobilized in cold storage,
watching ice crystals bloom on the
walls, a frozen man dreams –
Hot restaurants appear where
steamy dishes reveal an image in
the lobster soup of a man on snow-
shoes, breath puffing from his
fur-lined cocoon as he shuffles
across the moonlit tundra of an-
other world, and the temperature
settles ...

all the way down the scale.

seasons

a poem of rebirth

Spring lays flowers at our feet
Summer cloaks us all with heat
Autumn burns with life and loss
Winter our window panes emboss

Joy, sadness, grief, love,
All these are seasons too,
But Christmas is the one
I found with you.